*Rejoice, exult for joy, for behold,
your God is coming to save you.*

(from Isaiah 35:4)

The Beautiful Story of Jesus: Published 2015 by the Incorporated Catholic Truth Society, 40-46 Harleyford Road, London SE11 5AY. Tel: 020 7640 0042; Fax: 020 7640 0046; www.CTSbooks.org Copyright © 2015 The Incorporated Catholic Truth Society in this English-language edition.

ISBN: 978 1 78469 082 3   CTS Code CH61

Translated from the French Edition by Helena Scott: **La belle histoire de Jésus** written and illustrated by Maïte Roche, published 2007 by Edifa-Mame, 15-27 rue Moussorgski, 75018 Paris; ISBN Mame 978-2-7289-1219-3; Edifa 978-2-9163-5011-0; Copyright © Edifa Mame - 2007.

Maïte Roche

The Beautiful Story of Jesus

According to the Gospels

*G*od sent the Angel Gabriel
to announce some wonderful news
to Mary, a young girl from Galilee.

He went into her house and said to her:
"Hail, Mary, full of grace, the Lord is with you.
God has chosen you to be the mother of his Son,
Jesus, the Saviour; the Holy Spirit will come
upon you." Mary accepted. She said:
"I am the handmaid of the Lord."

ary went to visit her cousin
Elizabeth, who was also expecting a baby:
John the Baptist.
When Mary greeted Elizabeth, John the Baptist
danced for joy inside his mother's womb.
Then Elizabeth, filled with the Holy Spirit,
understood that the baby Mary was expecting
was the Saviour.

She cried out: "Mary, you are blessed among women, and your child is blessed!"
Mary replied joyfully:
"God has done marvels for me!"

On the day of the wedding of Joseph and Mary, there was a big celebration in Nazareth. Joseph knew that Mary was expecting Jesus, the Son of God. He was going to love and protect Jesus like a father.

Jesus was born in Bethlehem.
He was laid in a manger.
Glory to God, and peace on earth!

It's Christmas! The shepherds were astonished.
A new star shone in the sky.
It guided the wise men who came from far
away to adore Jesus.

*J*oseph and Mary went to present Jesus in the Temple in Jerusalem.

The wise old Simeon took Jesus in his arms. Through the Holy Spirit, he realised that this little baby was the long-awaited Saviour. Full of joy, he exclaimed: "This is the light that will enlighten all nations!"

Jesus grew up in the house of Joseph and Mary in Nazareth. He was filled with wisdom and the love of God his Father.

hen Jesus was twelve, he stayed for three days in the Temple in Jerusalem with the wise men and priests. They were completely amazed at his intelligence and how he understood the word of God.

Joseph and Mary were very worried, and searched for him high and low. When they found him again, Jesus said to them:

"Why were you searching for me?
My Father's house is where I have to be."

John the Baptist grew up. He announced to everyone that the Saviour was coming. "Be converted, prepare your hearts, for the Lord is coming."

And he baptised them in the water of the River Jordan. When Jesus was baptised, the Holy Spirit came down on him like a dove, and a voice was heard saying: "This is my beloved Son, with whom I am well pleased."

eter and his brother Andrew, James and his brother John, were fishing on the lake. Jesus called them and said to them: "Come, follow me, I will make you into fishers of men." They left everything and followed him. Jesus also called Philip, Bartholomew, Thomas and Matthew, James the son of Alphaeus, Thaddaeus, Simon and Judas. These were the twelve Apostles.

great crowd came up the mountain to listen to Jesus. He announced the Good News for everyone: "Rejoice, the Kingdom of God is a Kingdom of love, where you will be happy forever. God welcomes the poor and comforts those who are crying. Happy are the meek, they will possess the promised land."

"Happy are those who forgive, they will be forgiven. Happy are the peacemakers, they will be called God's children."

A disciple asked Jesus: "Lord, teach us how to pray." Jesus replied,

"When you pray, say:
Our Father, who art in Heaven,
hallowed be thy name.
Thy kingdom come,
Thy will be done on earth as it is in Heaven.
Give us this day our daily bread,
and forgive us our trespasses, as we forgive
those who trespass against us, and lead us not
into temptation, but deliver us from evil."

Lots of sick people came to Jesus, and he cured them: now the blind can see, the deaf can hear, the lame can walk again. One day, a paralysed man was even lowered through the roof of the house!

Jesus said to him: "I forgive you your sins. Get up, pick up your stretcher and go back home!" The paralysed man got up at once – he was cured! Lots of people started wondering: "Who is Jesus? He does things that only God can do!"

A huge crowd followed Jesus up the mountainside. It was evening, people were hungry, and they had nothing to eat. A boy brought five loaves of bread and two fish to Jesus: It was very little for so many people!

Jesus took the loaves, blessed them and broke them up, then he gave them out. He did the same with the fishes. After the meal, there were twelve basketfuls of leftovers. Everyone had enough to eat, and went home rejoicing.

*J*esus crossed the lake with his disciples.
A violent storm broke out,
and the disciples were terrified.
"Help, Lord, save us!" Then Jesus said:
"Why are you afraid, men of little faith!"
He rebuked the wind and said to the sea:
"Silence! Be quiet!" and everything
became calm. The disciples asked each other:
"But who is he? Even the wind
and the sea obey him!"

The disciples wanted to stop some children from coming to Jesus. Jesus didn't agree: "Let the little children come to me, the Kingdom of God belongs to them, and to people who are like them."

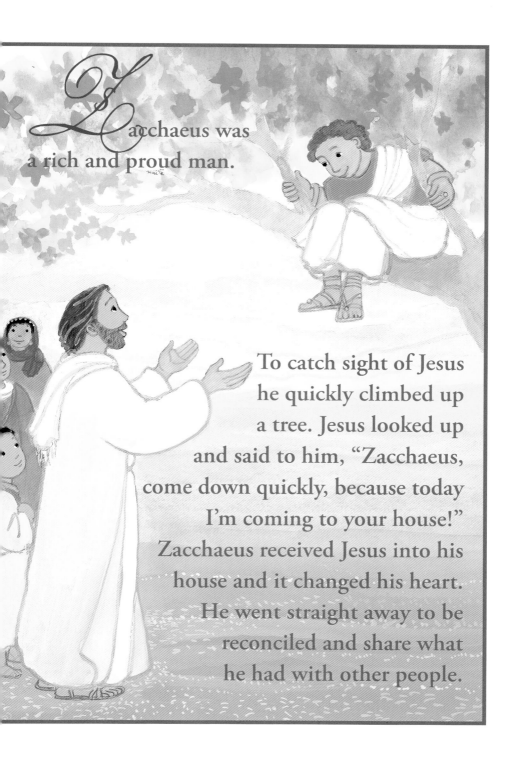

Zacchaeus was a rich and proud man.

To catch sight of Jesus he quickly climbed up a tree. Jesus looked up and said to him, "Zacchaeus, come down quickly, because today I'm coming to your house!" Zacchaeus received Jesus into his house and it changed his heart. He went straight away to be reconciled and share what he had with other people.

esus arrived in Jerusalem with his friends. He was hailed as a king: lots of people spread their cloaks on the road, others waved palm-branches and sang:

"Hosanna! Hosanna! Blessed is he who comes
in the name of the Lord!"

Jesus was teaching in the Temple. A scribe asked him: "Which Commandment is the greatest?" Jesus answered: "Love the Lord your God with all your heart, and your neighbour as yourself." But the leaders of the Temple had hard hearts. They wouldn't listen to Jesus, and they didn't believe that he was the Son of God. They wanted to arrest him and put him to death, but they were afraid of the crowd that surrounded him. In secret, they promised Judas thirty pieces of silver to help them arrest Jesus when he was alone.

*J*esus knew that Judas was going to betray him, and that he was going to die.

He gathered his Apostles together for a last meal. He wanted to prepare their hearts for all that was going to happen.

He knelt before Peter to wash his feet.
Peter refused to let Jesus, the Lord,
wash his feet like a servant. But Jesus insisted:
"Do what I do, serve one another and love
each other as I have loved you."

During the meal, Jesus took the bread and blessed it. He broke it and gave it to his friends, telling them: "This is my body, given up for you."

Then Jesus took the cup of wine, blessed it and gave it to them, saying: "This is my blood that will be poured out for everyone, for the forgiveness of sins to show my love forever."

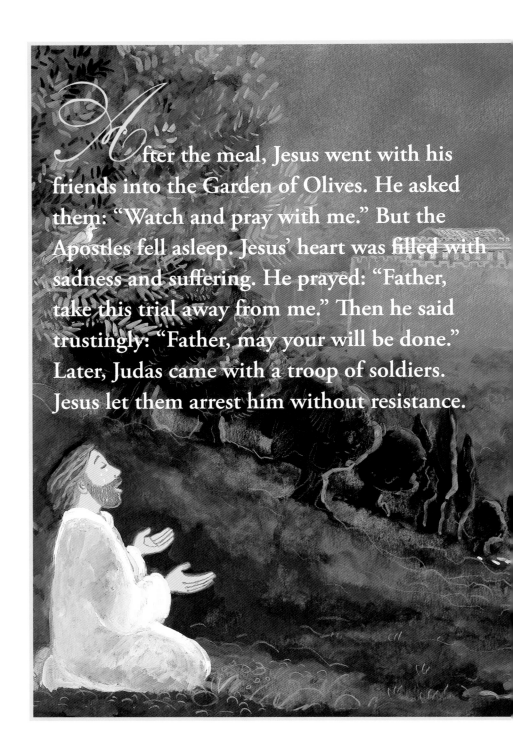

After the meal, Jesus went with his friends into the Garden of Olives. He asked them: "Watch and pray with me." But the Apostles fell asleep. Jesus' heart was filled with sadness and suffering. He prayed: "Father, take this trial away from me." Then he said trustingly: "Father, may your will be done." Later, Judas came with a troop of soldiers. Jesus let them arrest him without resistance.

Almost all the Apostles ran away because they were afraid. Peter himself would say three times that he didn't know Jesus.

The leaders of the Temple asked Jesus:
"Are you the Son of God?"
"I am," replied Jesus.

Then they led Jesus to Pilate,
the Roman ruler, to condemn
him to death. The soldiers
made fun of Jesus.
They put a red cloak on him
and a crown of thorns.

Pilate felt that Jesus shouldn't die, he had done nothing wrong. He said to the crowd, "Here is your king!" But they shouted, "Put him to death! Crucify him!" So Pilate let Jesus be condemned to death as a criminal.

*J*esus went along the way
carrying a heavy cross.

He was exhausted. So the soldiers forced
Simon of Cyrene to help him. In the crowd,
Mary was filled with deep sorrow as she saw
her Son suffering so much. Beside her was
John, the faithful apostle, and some friends
who were crying.

The soldiers nailed Jesus to the cross with two criminals, and then shared out his clothes. The crowd made fun of him. Jesus said: "Father, forgive them, because they don't know what they're doing." Mary, John and some women were standing at the foot of the cross. Jesus entrusted John to Mary, saying: "This is your son," and he entrusted Mary to John, saying: "This is your mother." And he prayed, "Father, into your hands I commit my spirit." Then he died on the cross. A great darkness fell on the earth. Seeing all this, the centurion said: "Truly this man was the Son of God!"

When evening came, the body of Jesus was taken down from the cross. Joseph of Arimathea had bought a great piece of linen cloth to wrap the body in.

Mary and the friends of Jesus were very sad.
They took Jesus' body into a tomb dug out of
the rock. A great boulder closed the entrance.

On Easter Sunday, early in the morning, Mary Magdalen, Mary the mother of James, and Salome went to the tomb to embalm the body of Jesus with perfumes and spices. When they arrived, they saw that the entrance to the tomb was open!

An angel of the Lord spoke to them and said:
"Don't be afraid, Jesus is risen, he's not here
any more! Go and tell his disciples!"
Jesus is alive! Alleluia! Alleluia!
Jesus' friends were filled with joy.

eter, John, and some others had been fishing all night without catching any fish. In the morning, they found Jesus standing by the lakeside, he said to them, "Throw the net to the right of the boat." Peter and his friends obeyed. They pulled in the net filled with big fishes. Then John recognised Jesus: "It is the Lord!"

Peter jumped straight into the water to go to
Jesus. Jesus prepared a meal with bread and fishes.
After the meal, he asked Peter three times:
"Do you love me?" Peter answered:
"Lord, you know everything, you
know that I love you." Then
Jesus chose him to guide all
those who believe in him: "You
will be the shepherd of my flock."

On the day of the Ascension, before returning to God, his Father and our Father, Jesus blessed his Apostles and made them a promise:

"You are going to receive the strength of the Holy Spirit and you will be my witnesses to the ends of the earth." And Jesus went up to Heaven and disappeared from sight. Then they went back to Jerusalem and every day, they prayed together with one heart, filled with hope.

On the day of Pentecost, the Apostles were all gathered together. Suddenly there was a violent gust of wind, and something like flames of fire came and rested on them: they were filled with the Holy Spirit.

They went straight out into the streets:
"Jesus is truly risen and he gives us his Holy Spirit!"
Everyone could understand them, even people who spoke a different language.

Three thousand people were then baptised in
the name of Jesus Christ. From that day on, the
Apostles and those who have come after them have
announced the Good News throughout the whole
world "in the name of the Father and of the Son and
of the Holy Spirit."

And know that I am with you always;
yes, to the end of time.

(Matthew 28:20)